Primary Sources of the Abolitionist Movement

Frederick Douglass and William Garrison
A Partnership for Abolition

Alison Morretta

Cavendish
Square
New York

Published in 2016 by Cavendish Square Publishing, LLC

243 5th Avenue, Suite 136, New York, NY 10016
Copyright © 2016 by Cavendish Square Publishing, LLC

First Edition

Cataloging-in-Publication Data

Morretta, Alison.
Frederick Douglass and William Garrison: a partnership for abolition / by Alison Morretta.
p. cm. — (Primary sources of the abolitionist movement)
Includes index.
ISBN 978-1-50260-532-0 (hardcover) ISBN 978-1-50260-533-7 (ebook)
1. Douglass, Frederick, — 1818-1895 — Juvenile literature. 2. Garrison, William Lloyd, — 1805-1879 — Juvenile literature. 3. Abolitionists — United States — Biography — Juvenile literature.
4. Antislavery movements — United States — History — 19th century — Juvenile literature.
I. Morretta, Alison. II. Title.
E449.D75 M67 2016
973.8'092—d23

Editorial Director: David McNamara
Editor: Amy Hayes
Copy Editor: Cynthia Roby
Art Director: Jeffrey Talbot
Senior Designer: Amy Greenan
Senior Production Manager: Jennifer Ryder-Talbot
Production Editor: Renni Johnson
Photo Researcher: J8 Media

The photographs in this book are used by permission and through the courtesy of: The Print Collector/Print Collector/Getty Images, cover; Ann Ronan Pictures/Print Collector/Getty Images, 5; Hulton Archive/Getty Images, 8; Richard Ellis/AFP/Getty Images, 10; MPI/Getty Images, 11; Archive Photos/Getty Images, 13; North Wind Picture Archives, 16; Stock Montage/Getty Images, 17; North Wind Picture Archives, 19; Boston Athenaeum, USA/Bridgeman Images, 21; Fotosearch/Getty Images, 23; Fotosearch/Getty Images, 25; Benjamin Hayden (1786-1846) File:The Anti-Slavery Society Convention, 1840 by Benjamin Robert Haydon.jpg/Wikimedia Commons 27; North Wind Picture Archives, 28; Everett Collection/Age Fotostock, 30; Southworth & Hawes (The Metropolitan Museum of Art), Public domain/File:John Quincy Adams - copy of 1843 Philip Haas Daguerreotype.jpg/Wikimedia Commons, 32; Library of Congress, 33; (top) Herbert Orth/The LIFE Picture Collection/Getty Images, (bottom) Stock Montage/Getty, 35; MPI/Getty Images, 36; George Peter Alexander Healy (1818-1894) File:G.P.A. Healy's portrait of John C. Calhoun, Charleston City Hall IMG 4589.jpg/Wikimedia Commons, 37; Library of Congress, 43; Library of Congress, 45; Francis Bicknell Carpenter (1830-1900) File:Emancipation proclamation.jpg/Wikimedia Commons, 47; Library of Congress (LC-USZC4-507) File:The Storming of Ft Wagner-lithograph by Kurz and Allison 1890.jpg (Public Domain) Wikimedia Commons, 48; American Photographer, (19th century)/Schlesinger Library, Radcliffe Institute, Harvard University/Bridgeman Images, 50; MPI/Getty Images, 52; Brady-Handy/Library of Congress/File:Frederick Douglass LOC collodion c1865-80.jpg/Wikimedia Commons, 53.

Printed in the United States of America

CONTENTS

INTRODUCTION • 4

A New Abolitionist Movement

CHAPTER ONE • 7

Abolitionists in the Making

CHAPTER TWO • 18

A Meeting of Minds

CHAPTER THREE • 31

The Nation Reacts

CHAPTER FOUR • 42

The Civil War and Beyond

Chronology • 54

Glossary • 56

Further Information • 58

Bibliography • 60

Index • 62

About the Author • 64

A New Abolitionist Movement

I n the years following the American Revolution, the principles of liberty and independence the colonists had fought for convinced the Northern states to gradually abolish slavery. However, in the American South, slavery was a thriving institution that brought a great deal of wealth to the slave owners. It was a part of their culture and crucial to their economy, and they were not going to give it up without a fight. To defeat such an entrenched institution, abolitionists would have to win over the hearts of the nation.

The abolitionist movement of the mid-nineteenth century was different from earlier antislavery efforts, some

Frederick Douglass and William Garrison:
A Partnership for Abolition

of which proposed **colonization** (the emancipation of slaves who would then be sent back to Africa to form their own civilization) and **gradualism** (the abolition of slavery over time

In this illustration, slave men, women, and children press and sort tobacco leaves on a plantation in colonial Virginia, circa 1750.

with compensation to slaveholders). The movement that existed from the 1830s until the end of the Civil War in 1865 was based on the idea of immediate emancipation of slaves, with no compromises or compensation.

The partnership between white abolitionist William Lloyd Garrison and former slave Frederick Douglass is one of the most important events in the history of the abolitionist movement. From the very beginning, Garrison was the leading (and loudest) voice in the movement. He worked tirelessly to promote the abolitionist cause and operated one of the most widely read abolitionist newspapers. Garrison recognized the potential of Frederick Douglass, who was incredibly intelligent and well-spoken. Together, these men accomplished what they could not do individually— Garrison was able to strengthen the movement by showcasing Douglass's abilities as a writer and **orator**, and Douglass was given a platform to speak for the millions of black Americans who did not have a voice.

Even though they would part ways after only eight years, their accomplishments as a team did a great deal to strengthen the movement and turn abolition from a small minority in the north into something that divided the nation and led to the bloodiest war ever waged on American soil.

Later abolitionists were also advocates of equal rights for black Americans, which was a new, controversial aspect to the movement. These activists fought hard to bring moral reform to a nation they believed was stained by the institution of slavery and the racial prejudice that allowed black Americans to be considered property and not people.

During the mid-nineteenth century, the main forms of mass communication were newspapers, books, and public speeches. For this reason, there is a wealth of primary source material written by the abolitionists, as well as the proslavery response. In order to carry their message across the nation, abolitionists wrote extensively in newspapers and toured the country speaking on the evils of slavery. When the organized movement began, the abolitionists were considered radical agitators. They had no political power or support, and their collective voice was their only weapon in the fight against the slave power of the South. They used it well, and often, and left a great deal of material to help modern-day historians understand what was happening in the nation at the time, and how they were trying to change it.

Frederick Douglass and William Garrison:
A Partnership for Abolition

Abolitionists in the Making

F rederick Douglass and William Lloyd Garrison
came from very different backgrounds. One was
born a black slave in the South and one a free
white man in the North. Both were self-made, self-
educated men. Their early hardships and dedication
to Christian morality shaped both and put them on
the path of becoming two of the most important
abolitionists in the movement.

Grandma Betsey's Cabin

The man we now know as Frederick Douglass was born
Frederick Augustus Washington Bailey in a small cabin in
Talbot County, Maryland. Later in life, Douglass estimated
that his birthday was around February 14, 1818, but for
many years he did not know how old he was. Frederick was

Slave women and children gather around a small cabin, circa 1850. Douglass lived in a cabin like this one as a young boy.

raised by his grandmother, Betsey Bailey, in a log cabin on the outskirts of Holme Hill Farm.

The windowless cabin had a clay floor and a dirt chimney, and the slaves slept on beds made from fence rails. Young Frederick had only a thin linen tunic to wear and was often cold. He took his meals on the floor and the food was "of the coarsest kind, consisting for the most part of cornmeal mush, which often finds its way from the wooden tray to his mouth in an oyster shell." The children rarely got enough to eat, and what they did get did not provide them with the proper nutrition for their growing bodies.

Betsy's five daughters had all been sold away from her, including Frederick's mother, Harriet. Harriet Bailey was a field slave at a plantation many miles away, and Frederick only saw her a few times before she died when he was around eight years old. To see her son, Harriet had to walk 12 miles (19.3 kilometers) after a full day of work. Slaves who overslept and arrived to the fields late were whipped, so Harriet could only stay for a short time before walking the twelve miles back, getting no sleep before another day working the field.

The only thing Frederick knew about his father was that he was a white man. It was rumored that his father was his master, Aaron Anthony. There were a large number of slaves with white ancestors, but the mother determined the child's slave status. The father "could sell his own child without incurring reproach, if in its veins coursed one drop of African blood."

Moving to "Old Master's" House

As a young child, Frederick was mostly unaware of the horrible conditions that other slaves lived in, but he was disturbed to learn that his home, as well as his grandmother and all the children, belonged to someone called "Old Master." Even worse, he learned that when the children got older, they were taken away to live with this unknown man. Douglass considered this "among the heaviest of [his] childhood's sorrows."

This "old master" was Captain Aaron Anthony. Anthony was an **overseer** at the nearby Wye House Plantation, owned by Colonel Edward Lloyd. The Anthony family lived in a house on Lloyd's plantation, 12 miles (19.3 k) from Holme Hill.

One summer day, when Frederick was six years old, Betsey Bailey walked the twelve miles with her

A house on the Wye House Plantation property on Maryland's Eastern Shore. The house, once owned by slaveholder Edward Lloyd, is now used for high-level political conferences.

grandson to the Wye House Plantation. When they arrived, Frederick saw a group of slave children and learned from his grandmother that among them were his brother, Perry, and his sisters, Eliza and Sarah. Frederick had never met his siblings and had no feelings toward them: "I heard the words brother and sisters, and knew they must mean something; but slavery had robbed these terms of their true meaning." After urging Frederick to go play with the other children, Betsey left her grandson at his new home. Frederick cried himself to sleep on his first night as a slave at the Anthony house.

From the Plantation to the City

When Douglass was around eight years old, he was sent to Baltimore to become the house slave of Hugh Auld. Life as a slave in the city was much different from life on the plantation. At the Anthony's, he had slept on the

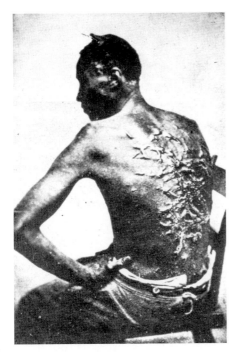

The brutal whippings that slaves received left many scarred for life, like this man from Baton Rouge, Louisiana.

cold kitchen floor with only an empty corn sack for warmth; in Baltimore, he slept on a bed of straw with a blanket. Instead of a thin tunic, he was given clean, proper clothes and shoes to wear.

Because such slaves would be seen out in the city, urban masters made sure their slaves appeared well cared for. In his *Narrative*, Douglass writes:

> There is a vestige of decency, a sense of shame, that does much to curb and check those outbreaks of atrocious cruelty so commonly enacted upon the plantation. He is a desperate slaveholder, who will shock the humanity of his non-slaveholding neighbors with the cries of his lacerated slave.

To protect their reputation in the community (which included many non-slaveholding whites) city masters were much more humane than plantation masters.

In Baltimore, Douglass had the opportunity to teach himself to read and write. Initially, Auld's wife Sophia

The Columbian Orator

Among Douglass's early reading materials was a book titled *The Columbian Orator* (1797), edited by Caleb Bingham. This anthology contained famous speeches, essays, and poems. It was used in American schools to teach reading and oratory. Douglass read it over and over, especially a section that contained a dialogue between a master and his slave. The slave, a two-time fugitive, is reprimanded by his master but speaks in his own defense. The dialogue lays out the arguments for and against slavery. The master is "vanquished at every turn" by the slave's argument and in the end he frees him.

Douglass studied that dialogue at a time when "every nerve of [his] being was in revolt at [his] own condition as a slave," and it made him want to seek his own freedom even more. This and other selections from the book "added much to [his] limited stock of language, and enabled [him] to give tongue to many interesting thoughts which had often flashed through [his] mind and died away for want of words."

(who had never owned a slave) taught him the alphabet. Auld forced her to stop, telling her that it was dangerous and illegal to educate slaves because it made them hard to manage and unfit for slavery. This was a turning point for Douglass. It taught him that "the white man's power to enslave the black man" was to keep slaves ignorant and "the pathway from slavery to freedom" was through literacy.

Douglass was determined to learn to read, but he had to be careful. With a basic knowledge of the alphabet from Mrs. Auld, Douglass made friends with some of the local white children. The children gave him reading

Frederick Douglass and William Garrison:
A Partnership for Abolition

When Frederick Douglass learned to write at a Baltimore shipyard, it was a thriving port city, as shown in this engraving of Baltimore's Patapsco River.

lessons in exchange for bread and he studied using any book or newspaper he could get his hands on.

By age twelve, Douglass was able to read quite well and wanted to learn how to write. He learned a few letters at the local shipyard by watching the ship carpenters labeling the lumber. Douglass then tricked local boys into teaching him new letters by challenging them to a contest: "[I] would make the letters which I had been so fortunate as to learn, and ask them to beat that if they could. With playmates for my teachers, fences and pavements for my copybooks, and chalk for my pen and ink, I learned to write."

A Man Unbroken

In March 1833, Douglass was sent back to Talbot County to live with Thomas Auld. Returning to a plantation after living in the city was difficult. In his new home, he again felt "the pitiless pinchings of hunger" and had to steal or beg for food. Thomas Auld was a cruel master, known to quote **scripture** while he whipped slaves and left them strung up and bleeding all day for minor offenses. Douglass hated how he was treated. He became difficult, often letting Auld's horses loose on purpose.

Auld was fed up and sent Douglass to work one year for Edward Covey, who was notorious for "breaking" slaves. Slave-breakers such as Covey took on slaves considered difficult to manage by their masters, and worked them as hard as possible. They doled out severe beatings and whippings. After a slave was broken, both physically and mentally, he or she became more agreeable and submissive and was then returned to their master.

Douglass suffered six months of hard field labor and constant whippings under Covey. By August 1833, Douglass had had enough. He refused to submit to a whipping and fought Covey for nearly two hours. Covey never whipped him again. Douglass considered this "the turning point in [his] career as a slave" that "rekindled the few expiring embers of freedom, and revived within me a sense of my own manhood." From that point forward, he was determined to escape.

The Road to Freedom

In Baltimore, Douglass had read stories about fugitive slaves and decided to escape. He tried to run away in 1835, but he and his accomplices were betrayed and captured. In 1838, he tried again. At the time, free blacks in Maryland were required to carry documentation of their freedom or they could be kidnapped and sold into slavery. Douglass's fiancé Anna (a free black woman) gave him a sailor's uniform to wear and he borrowed **free papers** in the form of a "sailor's protection"—a document issued to free black sailors to protect them from capture in Southern ports. Douglass secretly boarded a train. After a dangerous journey, he finally made it to New York City.

Even in the North, Douglass did not feel safe. He met another fugitive, Jake, who warned "there were hired men of my own color who would betray me for a few dollars … [and] men ever on the lookout for fugitives." An Underground Railroad operative named David Ruggles took Douglass in. Ruggles was a black abolitionist and member of the New York Vigilance Committee, which was dedicated to helping fugitives. Anna met him in New York, and it was at this time that he officially changed his name to Frederick Douglass. Ruggles helped the couple to New Bedford, Massachusetts—a New England town with a thriving abolitionist community. There Douglass would become acquainted with William Lloyd Garrison.

Growing Up in Poverty

William Lloyd Garrison was born in Newburyport, Massachusetts, on December 10, 1805. His father, Abijah, was an alcoholic sailor who abandoned Garrison and his mother, Frances Maria, when Garrison was three years old. Maria, very religious, was known as "Sister Garrison" in the community. Her strong Christian faith was a major influence on her young son.

Garrison did not have much formal schooling as a child because he had to work. Most of his early

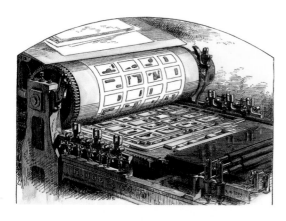

This woodcut print shows an early nineteenth-century printing press. Garrison learned the printing trade using machines like this.

education comes from the Bible, which was a constant fixture in his life and the inspiration for his fiery writing and speaking style. Maria could not support the family alone and young Garrison moved around a lot, often separated from his family. He was a lonely boy and was not fit for jobs that involved physical labor. In October 1818, at the age of thirteen, he found his calling when he went to work for the *Newburyport Herald*. As an **apprentice** to the editor, Ephraim Allen, he learned the printing trade that would eventually enable him to start his own paper.

From Apprentice to Editor

After his apprenticeship at the *Herald*, Garrison bought a local newspaper and named it the *Free Press*. The paper, however, was not successful and Garrison moved to Boston in 1826. While in Boston, Garrison was influenced by Lyman Beecher, a minister who was active in the Second Great Awakening religious movement. This movement emphasized that the way to salvation was through doing good works. Garrison went to work for a **temperance** newspaper, the *National Philanthropist*, where he developed his signature **editorial** style:

Frederick Douglass and William Garrison:
A Partnership for Abolition

aggressive, passionate, and controversial. Even early in his career, Garrison's writing had the ability to start heated debates.

The Editor Becomes an Abolitionist

In March 1828, Garrison met a Quaker abolitionist named Benjamin Lundy, who was in Boston to raise money for his newspaper, *The Genius of Universal Emancipation.* The more Garrison learned about abolition,

Benjamin Lundy

the more deeply committed to emancipation he became. One of Garrison's first major speeches, the "Park Street Address," which he made to members of the American Colonization Society (ACS), made it clear that the "monstrous inequality" between the races "should no longer be tolerated." He said that abolitionists should act "not by force, but fair persuasion." He gave his speech on the Fourth of July, and Garrison pointed out the hypocrisy of celebrating the nation's liberty while millions of Americans lived as slaves, exclaiming that "this is their country by birth, not by adoption. Their children possess the same inherent and unalienable rights as ours, and it is a crime of the blackest dye" to enslave them. Garrison had found his purpose in life, and the principles he put forward in this address would change very little throughout his life.

A Meeting
of Minds

William Lloyd Garrison used his publishing
skills and strong Christian beliefs to bring
about moral reform on the issue of slavery.
Garrison was always a controversial figure, never
compromising his beliefs or moderating his language,
but he ultimately found a large readership and became
a leading voice in the movement. One of his readers
was Frederick Douglass, and the two men formed a
partnership that turned abolition from a small Northern
minority movement into a nationwide issue.

Organizing the Abolitionists

The first issue of Garrison's abolitionist newspaper,
The Liberator, was published on January 1, 1831.

Frederick Douglass and William Garrison:
A Partnership for Abolition

In his inaugural issue Garrison wrote an editorial, "To The Public," in which he publicly rejected his initial support of gradualism and declared his commitment to immediate emancipation. He criticized the people of New England, where he experienced "contempt more bitter, opposition more active … prejudice more stubborn, and apathy more frozen" than that of the slave owners. He also made clear that he would not compromise his beliefs, declaring: "On this subject, I do not wish to think, or speak, or write, with moderation … I will not equivocate—I will not excuse—I will not retreat a single inch—AND I WILL BE HEARD."

Garrison knew that the abolitionists needed to organize if they were going to make progress across the nation. In 1831, he helped found the New England Anti-Slavery Society (NEAS). In 1833, he started a nationwide organization, the American Anti-Slavery Society (AAS), with the help of New York abolitionists Arthur and

Lewis Tappan. As the movement grew and more people started to read *The Liberator*, Garrison became the most well known and outspoken of all the abolitionists.

Garrison spoke at the December 1833 meeting of the AAS in Philadelphia. His speech, the "Declaration of the National Anti-Slavery Convention," states the beliefs of the organization:

> There is no difference, *in principal*, between the African slave trade and American slavery … every American citizen, who retains a human being in involuntary bondage, is a MAN-STEALER … the slaves ought instantly to be set free, and brought under the protection of law.

Garrison based his beliefs on his Christian faith and the rights of equality and liberty set forth in the Declaration of Independence. He went on to state, that all laws "admitting the right of slavery, are therefore before God utterly null and void."

The purpose of this speech was to lay out the position of the AAS: to reject the proslavery Constitution, to expand the organization across the nation, to speak on abolition and circulate antislavery literature, to purify the churches that supported slavery, and to achieve equality for black Americans.

Forming a Partnership

New Bedford, Massachusetts, was a community made up of abolitionists and other free blacks. It was there

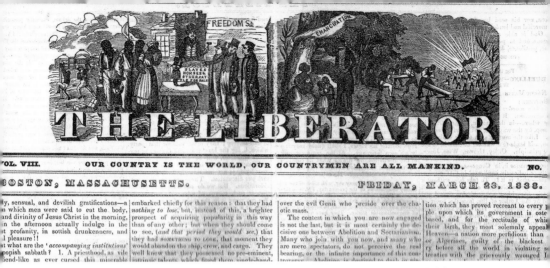

FREEDOM St.

EMANCIPATION

THE LIBERATOR

VOL. VIII.   OUR COUNTRY IS THE WORLD, OUR COUNTRYMEN ARE ALL MANKIND.   NO.

BOSTON, MASSACHUSETTS.   FRIDAY, MARCH 23, 1838.

ly, sensual, and devilish gratifications—a which men were said to eat the body, and divinity of Jesus Christ in the morning, n the afternoon actually indulge in the st profanity, in sottish drunkenness, and l pleasure!! at what are the 'accompanying institutions' popish sabbath? 1. A priesthood, as vile iend-like as ever cursed this miserable

embarked chiefly for this reason: that they had nothing to lose, but, instead of this, a brighter prospect of acquiring popularity in this way than of any other; but when they should come to see, (and that period they would see,) that they had somewhat to lose, that moment they would abandon the ship, crew, and cargo. They well knew that they possessed no pre-eminent, intrinsic talents which fitted them single-hand-

over the evil Genii who preside over the chaotic mass. The contest in which you are now engaged is not the last, but it is most certainly the decisive one between Abolition and Sectarianism. Many who join with you now, and many who are mere spectators, do not perceive the real bearing, or the infinite importance of this controversy.

tion which has proved recreant to every ple upon which its government is oste based, and for the rectitude of whi Heaven—a nation more solemnly appea their birth, they most solemnly appeal or Algerines, guilty of the blackest ry before all the world in violating s treaties with the grievously wronged I

The heading of this 1838 edition of *The Liberator* shows a slave child at auction. The masthead reads: "Our country is the world, our countrymen are all mankind."

that Douglass first read *The Liberator*. He wrote that Garrison's paper "took a place in my heart second only to the Bible" and that he "loved this paper and its editor" who was "an all-sufficient match to every opponent, whether they spoke in the name of the law or the gospel." Douglass became an avid reader of *The Liberator* and began attending local antislavery lectures.

Douglass had only the most basic understanding of abolitionism, but over the course of his first three years in New Bedford he became familiar with the principles of the movement. As he read Garrison and the other abolitionists, his "hope for the ultimate freedom of my race increased." At first, he was content to just listen and absorb information. According to the Fugitive Slave Law, because Douglass had escaped from his master he was a fugitive, and though he had spoken during meetings at his all-black church, he did not believe he could become a public advocate for the cause.

In the summer of 1841, Douglass was invited to speak at an antislavery convention in Nantucket, Massachusetts, organized by Garrison. About having never spoken freely in front of a mixed audience before, Douglass wrote: "I felt myself a slave, and the idea of speaking to white people weighed me down." Despite his hesitation, he gave a moving speech about his early life. This was the first time most white abolitionists had heard about slavery from someone who had lived it. The audience was shocked and impressed.

After hearing Douglass speak, Garrison hired him as a lecturer for the Massachusetts branch of the AAS. Douglass lectured all around the state but he soon grew tired of simply repeating his story. He felt restricted by the organization: "It did not entirely satisfy me to *narrate* wrongs—I felt like *denouncing* them … I was growing and needed room." It was not long before Douglass started to speak on larger issues that, until then, had only been addressed by the white abolitionists.

On December 23, 1841, Douglass gave a speech at the Plymouth Church Anti-Slavery Society meeting. From this speech, "The Church and Prejudice," it is clear that within a few months of joining the AAS, Douglass was already speaking his mind. He talked about his experiences of racial discrimination in the Northern church and the hypocrisy of Southern ministers. Douglass was not hesitant to express his outrage at the treatment black Americans suffered at the hands of white people, both Southern and Northern: "You degrade us, and then ask why we are degraded—you shut our mouths,

Frederick Douglass and William Garrison:
A Partnership for Abolition

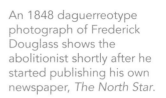

An 1848 daguerreotype photograph of Frederick Douglass shows the abolitionist shortly after he started publishing his own newspaper, *The North Star.*

and then ask why we don't speak—you close your colleges and seminaries against us, and then ask why we don't know more." Much like Garrison, from the very beginning of his career as an orator, Douglass made it clear that he would not moderate his voice or his beliefs on the issue of slavery.

"One Hundred Conventions" and Publication of the *Narrative*

Douglass experienced racial prejudice while lecturing in the free states on the "One Hundred Conventions" tour of 1843, but he also started to see that there was racism inside the AAS organization. At one meeting, he was reprimanded for "insubordination," which was a "strange and distressing revelation" for him. Douglass expected prejudice from people outside the organization, but he was disturbed and disappointed by the treatment he was receiving from some white abolitionists.

The Latimer Case

On October 4, 1842, George Latimer escaped from bondage in Norfolk, Virginia. Latimer was captured and arrested in Boston, outraging both the black community and white abolitionists. Douglass wrote Garrison a letter, published in *The Liberator*, in which he points out the hypocrisy of Christian patriots enforcing slavery.

> And all this is done in Boston—liberty-loving, slavery-hating Boston … Henceforth we need not portray to the imagination of northern people, the flying slave making his way through thick and dark woods of the South … but refer to the streets of Boston, made dark and dense by crowds of professed Christians.

Though Latimer was **manumitted** (voluntarily released by his master) in 1842, his case is important because it brought slavery to the attention of Northerners who had previously considered it a Southern problem.

Garrison fully supported Douglass and encouraged him to write his life story. Because Douglass was so intelligent and well spoken, many whites refused to believe he had been a slave. Douglass wrote his first **autobiography** as a response to this criticism, revealing personal details about his life that put him in danger of being captured. Thomas Auld was still his legal owner, and he could legally claim Douglass at any time. Despite the risk, Douglass wanted to tell his story and silence his critics. Garrison published Douglass's first autobiography, *Narrative of the Life of Frederick Douglass*, in 1845 and publicly supported him in the book's **preface**. Garrison praises Douglass's intellect and shames those who believe in the "natural inferiority of those who require nothing

This photograph, taken around 1840, shows Douglass (*middle left*) at an American Anti-Slavery Society meeting. AAS meetings were open to men and women, both black and white.

This oil painting by Benjamin Robert Haydon depicts a convention of the British and Foreign Anti-Slavery Society to promote worldwide abolition. Many American abolitionists attended the convention, held in London in June 1840.

but time and opportunity to attain the highest point of human excellence."

The *Narrative* sold well, which was both good and bad for Douglass. He was finally able to express his views in his own words and represent his race on a national scale, but he was in great danger after revealing so much personal information. Garrison sent Douglass on a speaking tour of Great Britain and Ireland soon after publication, both to promote the book and to keep him safe from capture.

Equality Abroad

Douglass toured the United Kingdom from the summer of 1845 to the spring of 1847. He suffered racial

Frederick Douglass and William Garrison:
A Partnership for Abolition

discrimination on his voyage overseas: the ship was segregated and he was forced to stay in steerage while his white companion was allowed to stay in a passenger cabin. He was also harassed by proslavery men while giving a speech on the deck. These experiences made it more satisfying when he arrived in Liverpool, England, and was greeted enthusiastically by the British people. The United Kingdom of Great Britain and Ireland had abolished slavery in 1833, and the foreign abolitionists received Douglass warmly throughout his tour.

Douglass truly felt as an equal during his time abroad, as shown in a letter he wrote on January 1, 1846, to Garrison from Belfast, Ireland:

> I have spent some of the happiest moments of my life since landing in this country … the entire absence of everything that looked like prejudice against me, on account of the color of my skin [contrasts] so strongly with my long and bitter experience in the United States.

In Great Britain and Ireland he was "treated at every turn with the kindness and deference paid to white people." For the first time in his life, Douglass felt like a free man.

The Price of Freedom

In late 1846, Douglass's British friends purchased his freedom. This caused controversy among some American abolitionists who felt that exchanging money for freedom was accepting the fact that slaves were property.

Douglass was criticized for violating the principles of the abolitionist movement and many people wrote angry letters to *The Liberator*. Even though it went against his principles, Garrison fully supported Douglass's decision.

This marked an important period of change for Douglass and the beginning of the rift in his relationship with Garrison. Even though he supported Douglass, Garrison was and always would be a man of his principles. He understood the reasons Douglass wished to gain legal freedom, but he still believed that there should be no compromise with slaveholders. Douglass was more practical and willing to change his position on the intricacies of the issue to achieve his end goal. By this point Douglass had grown out of the role that he first played in the movement. He had initially accepted all of Garrison's abolitionist principles, but now he was thinking for himself.

A woodcut print shows Douglass giving a speech to British abolitionists while on his tour of Great Britain and Ireland from 1845 to 1847.

Douglass's British friends also encouraged him to start his own newspaper and had raised some money for

Frederick Douglass and William Garrison:
A Partnership for Abolition

it. This time, Garrison did not support him. Along with other members of the AAS, he discouraged Douglass from branching out on his own. The AAS believed it would hurt the cause if Douglass focused on his own paper instead of putting his energies toward the organization.

The Beginning of the End

By 1847 there was a middle ground forming on the slavery question in America: many Americans were against slavery spreading into new territory, but still held racial prejudice and did not support immediate emancipation. In this environment, Garrison and Douglass embarked on a speaking tour of Pennsylvania, Ohio, and New York in August 1847, to encourage these people to join the abolitionist cause. They lectured on "**come-outerism**," which meant that people should reject all organizations (both churches and political parties) that made compromises with slavery.

Garrison got very sick in Cleveland, and Douglass went on to the New York lectures alone. It took three weeks for Garrison to heal, and when he did he was very upset that Douglass had not contacted him during his illness. Even more hurtful, Garrison found out secondhand that Douglass was moving to Rochester, New York, and starting his own newspaper, *The North Star*.

The final split between Douglass and Garrison occurred at the May 1851 AAS meeting. Having run his own paper for a few years, Douglass had learned more about laws regarding slavery and formed his own opinions. He now believed that the Constitution was an antislavery

This photo shows an original copy of the front page of the June 2, 1848, issue of *The North Star*. Douglass started his own newspaper despite the objections of some white abolitionists.

document and that supporting antislavery political parties would be an effective way to bring about abolition. At the meeting, Douglass publicly rejected Garrison's views on the Constitution and the Union. He said that the Constitution should "be wielded in behalf of emancipation" and that it was "the first duty of every American citizen, whose conscience permits to do so, to use his political as well as his moral power" to fight slavery.

This was the final break in their friendship and partnership. Even though Douglass and Garrison maintained their respect for one another publically, by the mid-1850s, the two men who had done so much together to shape the abolitionist movement were no longer speaking.

Frederick Douglass and William Garrison:
A Partnership for Abolition

The Nation Reacts

The spread of abolitionist sentiment throughout the Northern states in the 1830s and 1840s was not received well. Both proslavery Southerners and prejudiced Northerners were very resistant to the ideas of immediate emancipation and equality. All through the nation, abolitionists were painted as radical agitators who were threatening the safety of the American people, the sanctity of the Christian religion, and the political union between the North and South.

Congressional Gag Rule

One of the first coordinated efforts by the AAS was a mail campaign in the summer of 1835 to spread abolitionist literature to the slave states. Southerners tried to suppress the material and state legislators passed

Massachusetts house representative and former US president John Quincy Adams, pictured in this 1843 photograph, spoke out against the gag rule on abolitionist petitions in Congress.

laws banning abolitionist publications. Many Southern postal workers refused to deliver them. In an extreme example of the Southern response, an angry mob in Charleston, South Carolina, seized all abolitionist literature from the post office and burned it. In December 1835, proslavery president Andrew Jackson urged Congress to pass a law prohibiting the circulation by mail of abolitionist literature in the Southern states, believing it would lead to slave revolts.

The AAS also flooded Congress with petitions calling for the abolition of slavery in the District of Columbia. In response, proslavery representatives enacted a **gag rule**, which meant that any petition regarding slavery could not be discussed or acknowledged by the House of Representatives. Massachusetts representative John Quincy Adams was one of the most vocal opponents to the gag rule. Adams was not an abolitionist, but he was antislavery and strongly believed in freedom of speech. He viewed the gag rule as a violation of the first amendment rights of the people and argued against it for years. The gag rule remained in place from 1831 until 1844, when Adams finally succeeded in getting it repealed.

Frederick Douglass and William Garrison:
A Partnership for Abolition

Anti-Abolitionist Violence in the North

The aggressive response was not limited to the South. Many prejudiced white Northerners were opposed to the idea of racial equality and the growing population of black people in the free states. The economy was also a contributing factor to proslavery sentiment. Northern textile manufacturing required Southern cotton, and there were many people who wanted slavery to continue so that the Northern economy was not disrupted. Even in the free states, abolitionists were subject to harassment, violence, and even murder.

The proslavery press often published reports of the abolitionists' activities and printed **handbills**

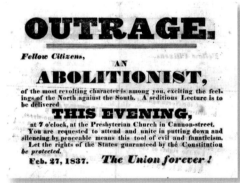

OUTRAGE.

Fellow Citizens,

AN
ABOLITIONIST,

of the most revolting character is among you, exciting the feelings of the North against the South. A seditious Lecture is to be delivered

THIS EVENING,

at 7 o'clock, at the Presbyterian Church in Cannon-street. You are requested to attend and unite in putting down and silencing by peaceable means this tool of evil and fanaticism. Let the rights of the States guaranteed by the Constitution be protected.

Feb. 27, 1837. *The Union forever!*

Anti-abolitionists in the North often published handbills, such as this one, which published details about local antislavery meetings and urged people to cause trouble.

urging people to take violent action against them. When British abolitionist George Thompson was scheduled to lecture at a meeting of the Boston Female Anti-Slavery Society, the following handbill incited the people to violence:

That infamous foreign scoundrel [George] Thompson will hold forth *this afternoon* at *The Liberator* office, No. 48, Washington Street. The present is a fair opportunity for friends of the Union to *snake Thompson out*!

It will be a contest between the Abolitionists and the friends of the Union. A purse of $100 has been raised by a number of patriotic citizens to reward the individual who shall first lay violent hands on Thompson.

This was just adding fuel to the fire already burning in Boston. There were already violent riots and lootings going on in the area of Boston with a high number of black residents. When Garrison spoke out against this violence, the mob put a **gallows** (a structure used to hang criminals) in front of his home as a symbolic threat of lynching.

On October 21, 1835, a group of citizens showed up at the meeting hall, but Thompson was not there. Garrison was, and he attempted to escape the mob by sneaking out the back of the hall. He was captured and dragged through the streets and the editor was forced to spend the night in jail for his own safety.

Douglass also experienced mob brutality throughout his career as a lecturer. While on the "One Hundred Conventions" tour in 1843, he was attacked at an outdoor meeting in Pendleton, Indiana. During the fight, Douglass's hand was broken and he was knocked unconscious. In 1847, Douglass was attacked again in Harrisburg, Pennsylvania, while on tour with Garrison, who described the incident in a letter to his wife, Helen. He told her that "mischief was brewing and an explosion would ultimately follow" and that when Douglass tried to speak, "the spirit of rowdyism began to show itself outside of the building." No black person had ever spoken

Frederick Douglass and William Garrison:
A Partnership for Abolition

Abolitionists were often subject to violence by proslavery Northerners. In the top image, an anti-abolitionist mob in Boston, Massachusetts, attacks William Lloyd Garrison in 1835. In the left image, Frederick Douglass is attacked at a meeting in Pendleton, Indiana.

publically in Harrisburg, and "it was regarded by the mob as an act of unparalleled audacity."

The mob threw bricks through the windows of the courthouse and pelted the people with rotten eggs. This extreme racial prejudice in a free city of the North was disturbing to the abolitionists, but attacks on freedom of speech and freedom of assembly were common responses by proslavery Northerners outraged by the abolitionists' ideas of disunion and racial equality.

Slavery As a "Positive Good"

From the beginning of the organized abolitionist movement in the 1830s, there was resistance on the part of proslavery Southerners who saw the abolitionists' cause

Elijah P. Lovejoy

The first martyr to the cause of abolition was newspaper editor Elijah P. Lovejoy. In July 1836, Lovejoy was driven out of St. Louis, Missouri, by a proslavery mob. The attacks on slavery and support of gradual emancipation Lovejoy published in his paper, the *St. Louis Observer*, angered many people in the slave state of Missouri. The mob destroyed his press and he relocated to Alton, Illinois.

Lovejoy started a new abolitionist paper, the *Alton Observer*. Alton was a border town on the Mississippi River across from St. Louis. Even though Illinois was a free state, it was filled with supporters of slavery, including slave catchers who made a living capturing fugitives coming across the river. Alton also had an active abolitionist community with stops on the Underground Railroad, and the tension between the two factions

An 1838 woodcut depicts the Alton, Illinois, riot, where a proslavery mob murdered abolitionist publisher Elijah Lovejoy and burned his printing press.

often erupted in violence. Lovejoy's printing press was destroyed three times and his home was attacked. Finally, on November 7, 1837, a mob set fire to the warehouse where his fourth press was and Lovejoy was shot and killed while trying to stop them. The murder of a white abolitionist in a free state caused many Northerners to join the abolitionist cause.

Frederick Douglass and William Garrison:
A Partnership for Abolition

as an attack on their economic and political power. The economy of the South was based on agriculture, especially cotton, which required a lot of labor. Southerners needed slaves to keep their plantations profitable, and they saw

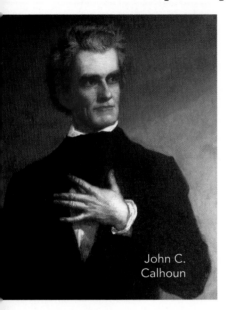

John C. Calhoun

abolition as a direct attack on their livelihood. The North also had a majority population, and as the abolitionist movement grew, there was concern that the government would ignore the minority interests of Southerners.

South Carolina senator John C. Calhoun, the son of a wealthy plantation owner, became the most influential representative of the slave power in Congress during the 1830s and 1840s. Calhoun supported states' rights and believed that, since the Southern states were a minority, they should have the power to reject any federal law they believed to be unconstitutional (a process known as **nullification**). Calhoun opposed abolition and any attempts to limit the expansion of slavery into new territory acquired by the United States.

Calhoun gave a famous speech to the Senate in 1837 in response to the abolitionists' petitions. Some Southern politicians had argued that slavery was a necessary evil, but Calhoun claimed the institution was a "positive good."

[The slave population] came among us in a low, degraded, and savage condition, and

in the course of a few generations it has
grown up under the fostering care of our
institutions, reviled as they have been, to its
present comparatively civilized condition …
I hold that in the present state of civilization,
where two races of different origin, and
distinguished by color, and other physical
differences, as well as intellectual, are
brought together, the relation now existing in
the slaveholding States between the two, is,
instead of an evil, a good—a positive good.

Calhoun's argument is based on his belief in the natural
inferiority of black people—a common prejudice held
in the North as well as the South. He points to the poor
living conditions of free laborers in the North and abroad
as an example of the benefits of the slave system, arguing
that Southern slaveholders always had the best interests of
their slaves in mind because mistreating them would make
them less valuable. This belief in **paternalism**, or the idea
that the masters are controlling the slaves for their own
good, was a common proslavery argument.

Biblical Justification of Slavery

Garrison and Douglass argued that slavery was a moral
evil and that no one could be a true Christian if they
supported the institution. Their frequent attacks on
Southern religion prompted proslavery Christians to
respond with arguments analyzing Biblical scripture.
Thornton Stringfellow, a Baptist minister from Virginia,
wrote "A Brief Examination of Scriptural Testimony

on the Institution of Slavery" (1841) as a rebuttal to the abolitionists' arguments that slavery went against Christian principles.

Stringfellow analyzed many passages from the Bible, including the story of Abraham. In the Book of Genesis, Abraham takes a second wife, an Egyptian "servant" named Hagar, because his wife, Sarah, is too old to have children and God has promised Abraham's descendants a kingdom. When Hagar runs away, the angel of God finds her and tells her to return and submit to Sarah. Stringfellow analyzes this story as it relates to American slavery and the abolitionist movement:

> Instead of ... heaping reproach upon Sarah, as a hypocrite, and Abraham as a tyrant, and giving Hagar direction how she might get into Egypt, from whence (according to Abolitionism) she had been unrighteously sold into bondage, the angel [of God] addressed her as "Hagar, Sarah's maid" ... (thereby recognizing the relation of master and slave) ... [Hagar] knew nothing of abolitionism, and God by his angel did not become her teacher.

Elsewhere, Stringfellow addresses the abolitionist argument that the term "slave" does not appear in the Bible (the word "servant" is used instead). Stringfellow argues that, because servants in the Bible are the property of men and can be bought and sold, they are no different than American slaves.

Resistance from Within

Over the course of his eight-year partnership with Garrison, Douglass felt increasingly limited and mistreated by some of the white abolitionists in the movement. He was disappointed that people who claimed to support the freedom and equality of the millions of slaves held in bondage were still clinging to racial prejudice, especially members of the Northern clergy who claimed to support the movement.

In August 1846, Garrison and Douglass attended the World's Temperance Convention in London. Douglass was asked to give a speech, which offended the American ministers in attendance, even those who did not support slavery. They believed that the issue of slavery had no place at a temperance meeting, but Douglass and Garrison believed temperance was a moral issue that affected all people regardless of race.

Reverend Samuel Hanson Cox from Brooklyn, New York, was especially displeased with Douglass's speech. In a letter to the *New York Evangelist* newspaper after the conference, Cox attacked Douglass for disrupting the convention and painting the American temperance societies as prejudiced. Douglass responded with a letter to Cox, which Garrison published in the November 27, 1846 issue of *The Liberator*. Cox had called Douglass's speech an "abomination" but left out details in his attack in the *Evangelist*. In his letter, Douglass gives the content of his speech, in which he said that he could not fully support the American ministers or temperance societies because they excluded black Americans.

This letter provides an excellent example of how the Northern clergy were as guilty as the Southerners when it came to sanctioning slavery. Cox claimed to be an abolitionist yet did not support Douglass speaking at the meeting, and Douglass attacked him for his hypocrisy.

> Sir, you claim to be a Christian, a philanthropist, and an abolitionist. Were you truly entitled to any one of those names, you would have been delighted at seeing one of Africa's despised children … warmly welcomed to a world's temperance platform, and in every way treated as a man and a brother.

Douglass criticized Cox for making him seem like an intruder at a meeting which "was not a *white* temperance meeting, such are held in the United States, but a 'world's temperance meeting,' embracing the black as well as the white." Douglass makes it clear that he was not paid or acting on behalf of anyone else, but simply exercising his right to speak on behalf of the millions of American slaves who did not have a voice.

The Civil War and Beyond

During the presidential campaign of 1860, several Southern states threatened secession if Republican candidate Abraham Lincoln was victorious. After decades of tension between the North and South, Lincoln's election was the last straw for many Southerners. South Carolina led the charge, and within three months of the election, seven Southern states had seceded from the Union and formed the Confederate States of America. The Civil War began on April 12, 1861, when a Confederate militia attacked the Union-occupied Fort Sumter in Charleston Harbor, South Carolina.

Frederick Douglass and William Garrison:
A Partnership for Abolition

The image of Abraham Lincoln on the five-dollar bill is based on this 1864 presidential portrait, photographed by Anthony Berger.

Garrison Supports the War

Throughout Garrison's career he was a pacifist who had never supported political parties or candidates, and he had actively refused to vote. However, when the war began, he came out in favor of Lincoln and the Union. In supporting the war, he went against his belief in nonviolence, but he truly felt that the nation had reached the point of no return and that the war was God's punishment for the sin of slavery. Garrison firmly believed that slavery was the cause of war and that a Union victory would end in its abolition. He was able to rationalize supporting the war as a necessary evil to end slavery.

Garrison was initially patient with Lincoln, even though he felt that the president was not taking a strong enough stand against slavery. Lincoln believed slavery was a moral evil and opposed its extension into the territories, but he was not an abolitionist. He believed it was his duty to uphold the constitution, which legally sanctioned slavery in the South. He also rejected immediate emancipation in favor of colonization and gradual emancipation (with compensation for slaveholders), and believed that saving the Union was more important than freeing the slaves.

Just days after the war began, Garrison wrote a letter to his friend, Oliver Johnson, and said that it was not the time for "minute criticism of Lincoln," who was one of the "instruments in the hands of God to ... help achieve the great object of emancipation." But when the nation entered its second year of war, Garrison grew more critical of Lincoln's continued refusal to recognize that slavery was the war's true cause. He was receiving correspondence from British abolitionists questioning Lincoln and the North's goals in the war. In a letter to Johnson in September 1862, Garrison admitted that he was "skeptical as to the 'honesty' of Lincoln" and called him "nothing better than a wet rag." Garrison believed that Lincoln was being controlled by the "satanic democracy of the North" and "traitorous 'loyalty' of the Border States."

Garrison used *The Liberator* (for which Lincoln's White House had a paid subscription) to call for action on the part of the president to use his wartime powers

Frederick Douglass and William Garrison: A Partnership for Abolition

This 1943 mural by William Edouard Scott depicts Frederick Douglass meeting with Abraham Lincoln during the Civil War and urging the president to allow black men to enlist in the Union army.

to emancipate all slaves. He asked his readers to petition Congress and the president to take action.

Douglass Criticizes Lincoln

In the early years of war, the political climate was shifting toward support for abolition over preservation of the Union, and Douglass's voice was influential with antislavery politicians. Douglass was not moderate in his demands. He believed that it was Lincoln's responsibility to acknowledge that the war was about slavery, emancipate all slaves, and allow blacks to serve in the military. Douglass was insistent that, by serving in the war as equals, black soldiers would demonstrate their patriotism and humanity, and that whites would begin to accept the idea of racial equality.

Unlike Garrison, Douglass was able to personally influence Lincoln's wartime policies. He had the ear of antislavery politicians who found Garrison too fanatical, and the president greatly respected him. Still, Douglass was initially very critical of the president's policies, which he felt were not strong enough. Douglass believed that immediate emancipation of all slaves should be the primary goal of the war.

In September 1862, Douglass wrote a scathing attack on Lincoln in his paper, *Douglass' Monthly*. "The President and His Speeches" was published in response to the president's meeting with a group of black leaders, where he proposed a policy of colonization. Lincoln expressed the racist view common at the time: the two races could not live together and the solution was for black people to leave the country. Douglass was outraged and saw Lincoln as a traitor to the voters who elected him. He called him a "representative of American prejudice and Negro hatred" and accused him of being "more concerned with the preservation of slavery, and the favor of the Border Slave States" than he was for the "principle of justice and humanity."

The Emancipation Proclamation

By mid-1862, it made sense, both politically and militarily, to free all the slaves held in the Confederate states. The North had suffered several defeats, and freeing the rebels' slaves would weaken the Confederate

Frederick Douglass and William Garrison:
A Partnership for Abolition

army and strengthen the Union. Lincoln first presented the Emancipation Proclamation to his cabinet on July 22, 1862. It took effect on January 1, 1863, freeing all slaves in the Confederate states and allowing all former slaves and free blacks to enlist in the Union army. From that day forward, "all persons held as slaves within any State or designated part of a State the people whereof shall then be in rebellion against the United States shall be then, thenceforward, and forever free."

This 1864 painting by Francis Bicknell Carpenter depicts the first reading of the Emancipation Proclamation by Lincoln and his cabinet in 1862. The Proclamation took effect on January 1, 1863, and freed slaves in all rebel states.

After the Emancipation Proclamation was issued, Douglass dropped his militant criticism of Lincoln. Douglass called the proclamation "the most important of any to which the president of the United States has ever signed his name." He believed that Lincoln's hesitance to make a decisive move toward emancipation would

This 1890 lithograph depicts the Massachusetts 54th regiment storming Fort Wagner on July 18, 1863, in Morris Island, South Carolina. Many black soldiers fought and died for the Union in this and other Civil War battles.

The 54th and 55th Massachusetts Regiments

In February 1863, the abolitionist governor of Massachusetts, John A. Andrew, authorized one of the first black regiments to fight in the Civil War. Over one thousand men from across the North and from Canada, as well as some from the South and the Caribbean, enlisted in the 54th Massachusetts Volunteer Infantry Regiment. Frederick Douglass's sons, Charles and Lewis, were among the first to enlist. There were so many recruits that a second black regiment, the Massachusetts 55th, was created. William Lloyd Garrison's son, George, was one of the officers in the 55th.

On May 28, 1863, the Massachusetts 54th paraded through Boston on their way to board a ship to South Carolina. Garrison and Douglass were both in attendance to see the regiment off to war. Even though they fought side by side for years, all the officers in the 54th were white, and they received $3 more per week than the black soldiers. Douglass spent much of the war advocating for equal pay.

Frederick Douglass and William Garrison:
A Partnership for Abolition

guarantee that he would not go back on his word: "The whole situation having been carefully scanned, before Mr. Lincoln could be made to budge an inch, he will now stand his ground."

This was a victory for the abolitionists, although it was not ideal. The Emancipation Proclamation did not free slaves in the Border States or in Union-controlled areas. Lincoln wanted to keep the Border States on the Union side and was attempting to work out a plan for gradual, compensated emancipation.

A Call to Arms

Douglass believed that military service would bring about racial equality and he worked tirelessly to get black men to enlist in the Union army. After the first black regiments were authorized in Massachusetts, he gave his famous speech—"Men of Color, To Arms!"—on March 2, 1863, in his hometown of Rochester. The speech was published in many Northern papers and distributed in pamphlet form as a recruitment tool for the Union army. Massachusetts did not have a large enough black population to fill the regiment, and Douglass helped enlist men from other states.

Douglass believed that a war "for the perpetual enslavement of Colored men, calls logically and loudly for Colored men to help suppress it," and declared that it was a time for action, not criticism. He told potential soldiers that it was their duty to help fight to free their brothers and sisters in bonds and show the nation that they deserved freedom and equality: "The chance is now

This 1894 photograph shows Frederick Douglass with his youngest son, Charles Remond Douglass. The younger Douglass served in the Civil War and later worked for the US Treasury Department.

given you to end in a day the bondage of centuries, and to rise in one bound from social degradation to the plane of common equality with all other varieties of men."

On August 10, 1863, Douglass met Lincoln in person for the first time. At a private meeting in the White House, Douglass "was never more quickly or more completely put at ease in the presence of a great man than in that of Abraham Lincoln." Lincoln treated him with respect as Douglass told him about his efforts to enlist black soldiers, and the president listened to Douglass's suggestion that black and white soldiers should receive equal pay, equal protection, and equal rewards for their service. Lincoln did not commit to any of these suggestions, and though Douglass did not agree with his reasoning, he had a great deal of respect for Lincoln's "tender heart" and "humane spirit."

Reelection and the Thirteenth Amendment

Lincoln knew that the Emancipation Proclamation was a wartime measure and that a constitutional amendment would be necessary to end slavery. In April 1864, the Senate passed what would become the Thirteenth Amendment for the abolition of slavery, but it was rejected in the House, which had a proslavery Democratic majority. Lincoln's reelection platform, which admitted slavery as the cause of war and called for an amendment to end slavery, made full-fledged supporters of both Garrison and Douglass.

Garrison joyfully attended the Republican convention in Baltimore where Lincoln was nominated. The president personally asked him to the White House, and on June 10, Garrison met with Lincoln to discuss the abolition amendment. Garrison wrote his wife, Helen, the following day with the conviction that Lincoln would "do all that he can see it right and possible for him to do to uproot slavery, and give fair play to the emancipated."

Douglass was also incredibly supportive of Lincoln's reelection. He met the president for a second time at the White House on August 19, and they discussed Douglass's efforts on behalf of the Union army and the idea of encouraging slaves to escape and enlist. Douglass attended the second inauguration speech and was invited to the celebration at the executive mansion, where "no Colored persons had ever ventured to present themselves on such occasions." When police tried to stop Douglass from entering, Lincoln personally demanded he be let inside. The president asked Douglass if he liked his speech, telling Douglass, "There is no man in the country whose opinion I value more than yours."

Endings and Beginnings

After the Thirteenth Amendment became law on December 6, 1865, Garrison believed that his work was done. He resigned from the AAS and on December 29, 1865, he published the final issue of *The Liberator*. In his final editorial, he wrote: "The object for which *The Liberator* was commenced—the extermination of chattel slavery—having been gloriously consummated," it was best to leave the rest of the work to those "with more abundant means." Garrison retired to Roxbury, Massachusetts, to spend more time with his family, and although not nearly as active as he was in his prime, he continued to advocate for reform. He supported the temperance movement, and voting rights for blacks and women until his death on May 24, 1879.

After slavery was abolished in 1865, when this photograph was taken, William Lloyd Garrison believed his life's work was done and retired from the movement.

To Douglass, the work was just beginning. He realized that abolition was the first of many steps to

After the Civil War, Frederick Douglass continued to advocate for equality for black Americans and fought for women's rights. He held positions in the US government during Reconstruction and continued to publish and speak.

achieving full citizenship and equality for black Americans and rallied support for the last two Reconstruction Amendments. The Fourteenth Amendment, ratified July 9, 1868, gave full citizenship rights to all people born in the United States, including former slaves. The Fifteenth Amendment, ratified February 3, 1870, gave voting rights to all black men.

Though his primary goal was voting rights for black males, he supported equal rights for women and was active in the women's suffrage movement. Douglass was active in the Republican Party and became the first black man to hold a political appointment in America, serving as the US minister to Haiti. Douglass is considered the father of the modern American civil rights movement who paved the way for other leaders with his belief in the promise of the Declaration of Independence: "that all men are created equal, that they are endowed by their Creator with certain unalienable Rights, that among these are Life, Liberty and the pursuit of Happiness."

Chronology

Dates in green pertain to events discussed in this volume.

1619 The African slave trade begins in North America.

1789 US Constitution goes into effect.

1777–1804 Slavery is abolished in the northern states.

1805 William Lloyd Garrison born in Newburyport, Massachusetts.

1808 The foreign slave trade is abolished by Great Britain and the United States.

1818 Garrison starts his apprenticeship at the *Newburyport Herald*; Douglass is born Frederick Bailey in Talbot County, Maryland.

1824 Douglass is sent to live at the Lloyd plantation.

1826 Garrison starts publishing the *Newburyport Free Press*; Douglass is sent to Baltimore to live with the Aulds.

1828 Garrison meets Benjamin Lundy and learns about the abolition movement.

1829 Garrison gives "Park Street Address."

1831 Garrison starts publishing *The Liberator*.

1833 American Anti-Slavery Society is founded in Philadelphia.

1834 Douglass fights off Edward Covey, resolves to free himself from slavery.

1837–1839 The Grimké sisters speak against slavery to overflow audiences in New York and New England.

1838 Douglass escapes from slavery in Maryland and settles in New Bedford, Massachusetts.

1841 Douglass speaks at an antislavery convention in Nantucket, Massachusetts; Garrison hears the speech and hires Douglass as a lecturer for the AAS.

1845 *Narrative of the Life of Frederick Douglass* is published; Douglass leaves America for speaking tour of Great Britain and Ireland.

1846 Douglass's British friends purchase his freedom.

1847 Douglass and Garrison go on a speaking tour of Ohio, Pennsylvania, and New York, which Garrison gets too sick to finish; Douglass moves to Rochester, New York, and starts publishing *The North Star*.

1849 Harriet Tubman escapes from slavery into Pennsylvania.

1850 US Congress passes the Fugitive Slave Act.

Frederick Douglass and William Garrison: A Partnership for Abolition

1851 *Uncle Tom's Cabin* runs as a serial in the abolitionist newspaper *National Era* in Washington, DC; Douglass publicly announces his split from Garrisonian abolitionists; changes name of *The North Star* to *Frederick Douglass' Paper.*

1852 Douglass gives famous "Fourth of July" speech; Stowe's complete novel, *Uncle Tom's Cabin*, sells millions of copies.

1854 Congress approves the Kansas-Nebraska Act; Garrison burns the Constitution and the Fugitive Slave Act on July 4.

1855 Douglass publishes second autobiography, *My Bondage and My Freedom.*

1855–1860 Harriet Tubman rescues freedom seekers and leads them from Maryland to Canada.

1856 Proslavery activists attack the antislavery town of Lawrence, Kansas; John Brown leads a raid on a proslavery family, which launches a three-month conflict known as "Bleeding Kansas."

1857 Supreme Court hands down decision in the *Dred Scott v. Sanford* case.

1859 John Brown launches an attack at Harpers Ferry.

1860 Abraham Lincoln is elected president; South Carolina secedes from the Union.

1861 Civil War begins.

1863 Lincoln's Emancipation Proclamation frees the slaves in Confederate-held territory; Douglass meets Lincoln and helps recruit black soldiers for the Union army; *Douglass' Monthly* goes into publication.

1865 The Civil War ends; President Lincoln is assassinated; The Thirteenth Amendment to the US Constitution abolishes slavery; Garrison leaves the AAS, publishes last issue of *The Liberator* on December 29.

1866 The American Equal Rights Association is formed. Its goals are to establish equal rights and the vote for women and African Americans.

1868 Fourteenth Amendment grants US citizenship to former slaves.

1870 Fifteenth Amendment gives black men the right to vote.

1879 Garrison dies in New York City on May 24.

1895 Douglass dies in Washington, DC, on February 20.

1896 A group of black civil rights activists form the National Association of Colored Women in Washington, DC. The group works to further civil rights for blacks and obtain the vote for women.

Glossary

apprentice A person who has agreed to work for a specific amount of time in order to learn a trade from an expert.

autobiography The story of a person's life as written by that person.

colonization A racist approach to abolition that would free the slaves on the condition that they move to the African colony of Liberia to form their own civilization.

come-outerism The Garrisonian belief that people should reject all institutions (political and religious) because they did not support abolition.

editorial A newspaper or magazine article written by the editor that expresses his or her opinions and beliefs.

free papers A document used to identify Northern blacks as legally free, that included their personal information and a physical description.

gag rule A rule, regulation, or law that prohibits an issue from being discussed or debated.

gallows A structure used to execute criminals by hanging.

gradualism An approach to abolition that would free slaves over time and compensate the slave owners for loss of property.

handbill A small printed document (usually a notice or an advertisement) that is distributed to people by hand.

manumission The act of a slave owner voluntarily freeing his or her slaves.

nullification The Southern states' refusal to recognize federal laws with which they did not agree.

orator A highly skilled public speaker.

overseer A plantation manager responsible for controlling the slave laborers, often through physical violence.

paternalism The belief that slave owners protect and care for their slaves like a father cares for his family, but do not allow them any personal choices or freedoms.

preface An introduction to a book that states the subject and purpose of the work.

scripture The sacred text of Christianity contained in the Bible.

temperance The practice of abstaining from alcohol or drinking in moderation.

Further Information

Books

Elliot, Henry. *Frederick Douglass: From Slavery to Statesman.* New York: Crabtree Publishing, 2009.

Ferrell, Claudine L. *The Abolitionist Movement.* Westport, CT: Greenwood Press, 2007.

Lowance, Mason, ed. *Against Slavery: An Abolitionist Reader.* New York: Penguin Books, 2000.

McNeese, Tim. *The Abolitionist Movement: Ending Slavery.* New York: Chelsea House, 2007.

Thomas, William David. *William Lloyd Garrison: A Radical Voice Against Slavery.* New York: Crabtree Publishing, 2009.

Frederick Douglass and William Garrison:
A Partnership for Abolition

American Experience: The Abolitionists
www.pbs.org/wgbh/americanexperience/films/abolitionists

Experience the world of the abolitionists through historical reenactments and commentary by historians in this PBS documentary. Explore bonus content, interactive maps, and further resources relating to the film's subject.

Digital History: Pre-Civil War Era
www.digitalhistory.uh.edu/era.cfm?eraid=5&smtid=1

Conduct research, analyze primary sources, and draw your own conclusions about pre-Civil War history through the Digital History explorations page.

Digital History: Slavery
www.digitalhistory.uh.edu/era.cfm?eraID=6&smtid=1

Explore slavery's origins and its impact on American culture, economics, and politics.

Bibliography

Cain, William E., ed. *William Lloyd Garrison and the Fight Against Slavery: Selections from* The Liberator. Boston: Bedford/St. Martin's, 1995.

Douglass, Frederick. *Life and Times of Frederick Douglass.* New York: Collier Books, 1962.

————. *My Bondage and My Freedom.* New York: Penguin Books, 2003.

————. *Narrative of the Life of Frederick Douglass.* New York: Dover Publications, 1995.

Ferrell, Claudine L. *The Abolitionist Movement.* Westport, CT: Greenwood Press, 2006.

Foner, Philip S., ed. *Frederick Douglass: Selected Speeches and Writings.* Chicago: Lawrence Hill Books, 1999.

Garrison, William Lloyd. "The Liberator, October 24, 1835." *Fair Use Repository.* Accessed January 5, 2015. fair-use.org/the-liberator/1835/10/24/the-liberator-05-43.pdf.

————. "My Second Baltimore Trial." *Fair Use Repository.* Accessed January 5, 2015. fair-use.org/the-liberator/1831/01/01/my-second-baltimore-trial.

Lowance, Mason, ed. *Against Slavery: An Abolitionist Reader.* New York: Penguin Books, 2000.

Frederick Douglass and William Garrison: A Partnership for Abolition

Mayer, Henry. *All on Fire: William Lloyd Garrison and the Abolition of Slavery.* New York: W. W. Norton & Company, 1998.

Merrill, Walter M., ed. *The Letters of William Lloyd Garrison: Let the Oppressed Go Free, 1861–1867.* Vol. V. Cambridge, MA: Harvard University Press, 1979.

"Pro- and Antislavery Arguments and Conflicts (1840–1851)." *Teaching American History for Students.* Accessed January 5, 2015. americanhistory. unomaha.edu//module_display.php?mod_id=127&review=yes#1224.

Rapley, Rob. "American Experience: The Abolitionists." PBS video, 2:34. Boston, MA: WBGH Productions, 2013. Accessed January 5, 2015. www.pbs.org/wgbh/americanexperience/films/abolitionists/player.

Risley, Ford. *Abolition and the Press: The Moral Struggle Against Slavery.* Evanston, IL: Northwestern University Press, 2008.

Tillery, Tyrone. "The Inevitability of the Douglass-Garrison Conflict." *Phylon* 37 (1976): 137–149.

Trotman, C. James. *Frederick Douglass: A Biography.* Santa Barbara, CA: ABC-CLIO, 2011.

Index

Page numbers in **boldface** are illustrations. Entries in **boldface** are glossary terms.

abolitionist, 4–7, 15, 17–24, **19**, **23**, **26**, 27–33, **28**, **30**, **32–33**, 35–37, **35–36**, 39–41, 43–45, 48–49, 51
Adams, John Quincy, 32, **32**
  See also gag rule
Alton Observer, 36
American Anti-Slavery Society, 19–20, 22–23, **25**, 29, 31–32, 52
Anthony, Aaron, 9–10
apprentice, 16
apprenticeship, 16, 54
Auld, Hugh, 10, 12
Auld, Sophia, 11–12
Auld, Thomas, 13–14, 25
autobiography, 25, 55

Bailey, Betsy, 8–9
Bailey, Harriet, 8
Beecher, Lyman, 16
Boston Female Anti-Slavery Society, 33

British and Foreign Anti-Slavery Society, **26**
Calhoun, John C., 37–38, **37**
colonization, 5, 17, 44, 46
Columbian Orator, 12
come-outerism, 29
Covey, Edward, 14
  See also slave-breaker

Douglass' Monthly, 46

editorial, 16, 19, 52
Emancipation Proclamation, 47, **47**, 49, 51

free papers, 15
Free Press, 16
Fugitive Slave Law, 21

gag rule, 32, **32**
gallows, 34
Genius of Universal Emancipation, 17
gradualism, 5, 19

handbill, 33, **33**

Jackson, Andrew, 32

Frederick Douglass and William Garrison: A Partnership for Abolition

Latimer, George, 24
Liberator, 18, **19**, 20–21, **21**, 24, 28, 33, 40, 44, 52
Lloyd, Edward, 9, **10**
Lovejoy, Elijah P., 36, **36**
Lundy, Benjamin, 17, **17**
lynching, 34
   See also gallows

manumission, 24

Narrative of the Life of Frederick Douglass, 11, 25–26
National Philanthropist, 16
New England Anti-Slavery Society, 19
New York Evangelist, 40
Newburyport Herald, 16
North Star, **23**, 29, **30**
nullification, 37

One Hundred Conventions, 33–34
orator, 5, 12, 23
overseer, 9

paternalism, 38
plantation, **5**, 8–9, 37
   profit from, 37

Wye House Plantation, 9–11, **10**, 13
preface, 25

scripture, 14, 38
slave-breaker, 14
speeches
   "Church and Prejudice, The," 22
   "Declaration of the National Anti-Slavery Convention," 20
   "Men of Color, To Arms," 49
   "Park Street Address," 17
St. Louis Observer, 36
Stringfellow, Thornton, 38–39

temperance
   meeting, 40–41
   movement, 52
   newspaper, 16
   platform, 41
   societies, 40–41
   white, 41
   World's Temperance Convention, 40
Thompson, George, 33–34

Underground Railroad, 15, 36

About the Author

ALISON MORRETTA holds a Bachelor of Arts in English and creative writing from Kenyon College in Gambier, Ohio, where she studied the literature and history of antebellum America. She has written a number of nonfiction titles for middle and high school students on subjects such as American history, literature, and Internet safety. She lives in New York City with her loving husband, Bart, and their rambunctious Corgi, Cassidy.